LAST CARAVAN

LAST CARAVAN

Touring Afghanistan During
the 1978 April Revolution

by
Penelope Rundle

Gray Dog Press

Gray Dog Press
Spokane, Washington
www.GrayDogPress.com

Printed in the United States of America

Publisher's Cataloging-in-Publication Data

Rundle, Penelope
    Last Caravan:
    Touring Afghanistan During the 1978 April Revolution
    Includes bibliographical references
1. Afghanistan History. 2. Travel. 3. Culture. I. Title
Library of Congress Control Number: 200944114

ISBN: 978-1-936178-05-6

Editor's Note

This journal, written by Penelope Rundle, is a firsthand account of a 1978 tour. The text has been transcribed and edited from the original handwritten notebook.

Following this journal is an overview of the history of Afghanistan including the date of the incident described in this writing. In this overview, the reader can see Afghanistan has been embroiled by war, famine, political unrest, and military takeover for thousands of years. From its origins as a major trade route to the home of the Taliban today, Afghanistan has been, and will be, an important country geographically and politically.

Preface

In 1976, my husband volunteered, with my approval, for a two-year assignment to Tehran, Iran. Douglas had just completed training at Brooke Army Medical Center and owed time to the Army for his Health Professions Scholarship to dental school. In this combined military and embassy assignment, he treated Americans working in Iran in the Army hospital facility in Tehran. I worked in various civilian jobs.

We rented a beautiful apartment from an Iranian family with whom we became friends and whose teenaged daughter I tutored in French and English. After two years in Iran, we had the opportunity to visit Afghanistan with a tour group composed of American military and embassy personnel. The trip was an opportunity of a lifetime, something we did not understand until we returned.

We both took photographs and I kept a journal of our visit. These items resided in a dusty box—an unofficial time capsule—until recently when I organized them. We were privileged to see a facet of Afghanistan at the end of nearly forty years of peace, and on the precipice of decades of war.

We cannot forget its stunning landscapes and hospitable people.

Penelope Rundle
Spokane, Washington

Contents

The Plan

In April 1978, my husband and I toured Afghanistan. I kept a journal during the planned seven days and six nights as well as the forced stay during a military coup. As far as I know, this was the only tour of Afghanistan offered by the United States military special services in Tehran.

Our group was composed of men and women working for the Tehran embassy, private contractors in Iran, and United States military personnel. On our return to Kabul from several days spent in the Afghani countryside, Russian MIG's (Russian-built fighter aircraft) were strafing the palace and blowing up the neighboring streets and buildings.

The original itinerary was as follows:

Afghanistan Tour
7 days and 6 nights

Saturday April 22nd
- Group arrival at Kabul Airport
- Transfer to the Kabul Hotel
- Morning free
- Lunch at the hotel
- Afternoon sightseeing
- Dinner at the Baghe Bala Restaurant
- Night at Kabul Hotel

Sunday April 23rd
- Early breakfast and departure for Djelalabad and the Khyber Pass
- Lunch at Springhar Restaurant
- Afternoon return to Kabul

Monday, April 24th
- After breakfast departure for Puli-Khomri
- Visit to the big Stupa and Buddhist Monastery of Takhte Rostam
- Lunch in Samangan
- Visit of Sorkh Qotal, the Zoroastrian Temple near Puli-Khomri
- Dinner and night in Puli-Khomri Textile Club

Tuesday, April 25th
- After breakfast drive to Bamiyan
- Picnic lunch on road, very difficult road but has beautiful scenery
- Afternoon arrival in Bamiyan
- Dinner and night in Bamiyan Yurt Hotel

Wednesday, April 26th
- After breakfast visit of the Buddhas
- Picnic lunch by the Red City
- Afternoon visit to the City of Noise
- Dinner in Balkh Restaurant
- Night at Bamiyan Yurt Hotel

Thursday, April 27th
- After breakfast return to Kabul, visit of Shibar Pass, Ghorband Valley
- Lunch, kabab at a typical Afghan chai-khana in Baghe Awghan
- Afternoon visit of Istaliff
- Dinner banquet in Golden Lotus Restaurant
- Night in Kabul Hotel

Friday, April 28th
- After breakfast transfer to the airport, return to Tehran

That was the plan.
The following is how it transpired.

View of Hindu Kush from Bamiyan cave

Day 1
Saturday
April 22, 1978

We arrived at the prearranged meeting place in the Tehran American Compound at 3:30 a.m. No one was there except a bus driver sleeping on his steering wheel in a smelly bus. By 3:45, people began to trickle in dragging their luggage. At 4:00 a.m., we boarded the bus and left for Tehran Airport, arriving there the mandatory two hours early to check in for Ariana Airline's flight to Kabul scheduled for 6:30.

Time dragged, especially with heavily armed troops roaming the corridors and concourses, eyeing us suspiciously. As always when I get up in the middle of the night for a trip, the plane was delayed. At 10:30, when I slipped off to the bathroom, the flight was called. We loaded quickly and took off in half an hour.

On the flight over withered and dry northern Iran, Afghanistan's territory continued the blinding glare of sun off land baked golden brown punctuated by sharp mountains culminating in the Hindu Kush—literally "kill Hindus." The land below knew nothing of distinctly carved borders on our puny maps.

Smiling stewardesses dressed in navy uniforms served a breakfast of omelets, Kentucky-fried tuna, croissants, Belgian jam, butter, cheese, orange juice and coffee or tea. Not bad for an airline I had never heard of until the plane showed up on the tarmac in Tehran.

Prior to landing at Kabul Airport, the flight attendants came down the aisle selling quarts of whisky, vodka and brandy, which seemed odd. We discovered on arrival in Kabul that Afghanistan, a Moslem country, is dry and alcohol of any description is not only hard to find, but very expensive.

We were met in Customs by our tour leader from Afghan Travel, Dr. Anwar (not his real name). We boarded a large bus with elaborate purple pleated curtains for the short trip to an unlisted, no-star hotel, although we pre-paid for a better place. The 41 tour members became immediately irate about the change in accommodations since we were all looking forward to staying in the Kabul Hotel as stated on our itineraries clutched in our sweaty hands. The Kabul Hotel was known to be a second-class, but picturesque, establishment within walking distance of some areas of interest. Tour members were also upset about the late arrival, which eliminated our "free" morning in Kabul. Finally, the rainy, depressing weather in the middle of a desert unstrung everyone. Springtime in Afghanistan.

We bussed out to a beautiful restaurant on a man-made lake above a golf course for a delightful lunch of brown rice cooked with raisins and shredded carrots, lamb and beef kebabs, salad, and sliced lamb with fried potatoes and carrots. With friends, my husband and I bought and shared a bottle of local red wine, although the recently applied label called the brew "Italian." The stuff was so murky we couldn't see through it—one grape away from vinegar. Now I understood the sale of alcoholic beverages before we deplaned. We originally thought the wine came with the meal, but the waiter charged us for the filthy stuff. We won't make that mistake again. Later we saw the waiter laughing at us and realized we had been scalped.

There was the tourist pause for photographs since the sun came out on a truly magnificent setting before we decamped for a mad scurry down Chicken Street, the local market where you can buy almost anything including the purest hashish in the world. Already the quest for souvenirs has raised its ugly head. Some of the tour members came specifically to shop, not to waste time on archeological sites. Because we were already behind schedule, our tour leader bowed to pressure and dumped the group off in town for shopping.

I hate shopping in a hurry in a place I don't understand. More scalping comes to mind. Still, we came away with a string of lapis beads and several semi-precious loose stones for under $10. The lapis strand is interspersed with some sodalite beads, but who cares. It's beautiful all the same.

Dinner tonight was another feast set out in the Baghe Bala (Hillside Garden) Restaurant, a former mosque converted into a magnificent eatery. In this drafty, ornate interior of heavily carved stone and wood with Moorish arches and inlaid frescoes, there was one set of salt and pepper shakers for the entire restaurant. The meal was much the same as today's lunch. It is unsettling to be consuming all these well-prepared delicacies and realize that the waiters are watching and are so very thin.

After dinner we walked in the surrounding gardens with a view overlooking downtown Kabul under a full moon.

Copper shop in Kabul

Day 2
Sunday
April 23, 1978

I was no sooner lathered under the shower than the water turned to ice, then scalded me. The water returned to freezing, congealing the soap on my head. My husband endured the same shocker but we came out clean.

Breakfast in the hotel dining room consisted of runny eggs, black, thick tea, jam, butter and "nun" (pronounced noon), the same as barbari bread in Iran. It is delicious flat, unleavened brown bread that predates the Bible.

We loaded and departed on the bus by 7:45 a.m., 45 minutes late for Djelalabad and the Khyber Pass. No matter what the plan, there are always people with personal agendas gumming up the works, and in this case, slowing everybody down.

The scenery along the route was exquisite. Waves of purple, gold and white spring flowers competed with carpets of lime-green grass, rice, or wheat. Blooming trees shed petals in the wind. Our tour group celebrated sunshine in a cloudless blue bowl of sky and an orgy of photographs taken from the moving bus. Kuchi people, a widespread tribe between Kabul and Djelalabad, posed unaffectedly for numerous pictures in front of their felt tents, herds of goats, sheep, cattle, and camels.

We passed through a rugged gorge and paralleled the Kabul River all the way to Djelalabad where we arrived at 2:00 p.m. Lunch was exactly like yesterday's meals. Dr. Anwar, our guide, told us that these were the best dishes representing Afghani cuisine. Qabili palow, rice with carrots and raisins, simmered in the juice remaining from cooked meat is outstanding. A woman who is familiar with the preparation told me that cinnamon, cloves, cumin, and cardamom give the rice and meat its unique flavor and aroma.

After lunch, we drove to the entrance of the Khyber Pass and walked to the Pakistani border. The pass is rugged and difficult in some areas but through much lower mountains than I expected. We took photos of a fortress on a hilltop at sunset. Wind whistled through rocks and dislodged miniature landslides, letting us know that calm appearances were deceiving. This area is historically notorious for death and calamity to conquering armies. Our guide informed us that conquerors do not stay long in Afghanistan.

Dinner was a slight variation of lunch with meatballs instead of kebabs and a spinach dish that I really enjoyed. We took pictures of the colorful table presentation and the whole staff came out to stand in the background. Afghani people, generally, have been friendly and kind.

Our rooms in the Springhar Hotel are large and clean with beautiful Bokhara carpets and ceiling fans. The hotel is beside the Kabul River in an unkempt but abundant rose garden. We strolled under the full moon while night creatures serenaded violently summoning us to the smaller, more overgrown paths. Sudden scurrying in the undergrowth reminded us that scorpions and venomous snakes abound by the river.

We turned in, bushed, preparing for tomorrow's early start for an exhausting drive back to Kabul.

Springhar Hotel banquet hall

Young men in border town

Day 3
Monday
April 24, 1978

Breakfast was at 6:30 and we were loaded on the bus by 7:00. Still we departed late. I don't know why. Maybe I'm being too fanatical about time in a country that really doesn't care about watches or clocks. I rarely see any. Seasons seem more important here.

We reached Kabul by 11:00 where the guide dumped the majority of members off on Chicken Street for another round of shopping. We remained with a splinter group that insisted on seeing the Kabul Museum where we viewed artifacts from Bamiyan to the west and Hadda near Djelalabad to the east. Real Khyber rifles and Maiwand jezails were lovingly preserved in this pleasant and well-maintained building while the rest of our tour group haggled for fake rifles and souvenirs on Chicken Street.

The Museum is dark—fancy lighting as in American museums is unheard of in this corner of the world—but contains unusual treasures dating back to prehistoric times, including what is thought to be the first stone statue in Asia. One can decipher a neolithic face scrawled on a three-inch tall cylinder while pondering civilization's endless spirals. Are we really more civilized today?

Back to Chicken Street at high noon to round up the tour for a seven-hour journey to Puli-Khomri. As usual already, we are late, this time caused by waiting 45 minutes for a tour member to purchase a carpet. The dealer would only accept cash so the tourist went to the bank and cashed $600 worth of $10 traveler checks, Meanwhile the group sweltered in the sun. When our tourist boarded the bus and apologized, there was silence.

The drive to Puli-Khomri was briefly interrupted by a pit stop. There are no bathrooms on the highways outside Kabul. This was literally two pits in a stone edifice located opposite the Baghe Awghan Bazaar. Everyone was bursting so we used the male and female pits even though the stench from pooling urine and feces was overwhelming. This would be the only "comfort station" for the rest of the day.

We had kebabs roasted on skewers over charcoal in a dingy establishment fronting the bazaar. For most of the tour members, this was a little beyond local color. Nevertheless, we ate hungrily, supplementing kebabs with hoarded snacks (Vienna sausage, beef jerky, nuts, candy bars) that we had been warned to bring for just such an occasion.

Back on the road, disgruntled, hungry passengers (those who had rejected the kebabs) turned mutinous and grumbling until we headed straight into a mountain pass on this one-lane road with a sheer plunge over the side. Silence enveloped the bus as people tried not to stare out the window at the vertical view. We climbed steadily, ears popping, to snowy peaks of breathtaking beauty. Some passengers pleaded for another bathroom stop because they had refused to use the pits at Baghe Awghan Bazaar. In truth, scurrying behind rocks and desiccated bushes seemed better than the previous "comfort station." The driver's assistant, a young Afghani boy in rubber flip-flops, khaki shorts and white cotton shirt, leaped out to investigate the possibilities of a gorge when rocks rattled down on the roof of the bus. We took off hastily in a deluge of gravel and fist-sized rocks with the assistant barely hanging to the door before he pulled himself aboard.

The driver stopped further along the road at another vista unfolding into the valley below us. Everyone scrambled out and found relief in the nearest dehydrated shrubs or behind boulders tumbled from the mountain above.

The pass was a dark tunnel at the summit of this portion of the Hindu Kush range, the historical barrier between Afghanis and their Hindu neighbors in Pakistan. Silent ski lifts hung spectrally in front of the passage where we stopped for photographs. On the other side, it was snowing, but we plunged quickly to the plain and glacier-fed river leading to Puli-Khomri. Traversing this terrain, it is easy to understand why Afghanistan has remained relatively independent and difficult to conquer.

In lavender twilight, the bus threaded through herds of karakol goats and spring lambs spread across the road with disregard for the random traffic coming through this area. It seemed inevitable that we would hit a frightened sheep as we sped around a blind bend in the road. Everyone in the bus lurched forward with the impact. The expression on the herder's face was tragic fury, shaking fists at our hit and run from the bloody scene. The driver did not stop to check for damages to the bus until several miles away. In fairness, the driver had narrowly avoided herds of animals all day and had almost circumvented the poor sheep until it turned and ran into the bus's right front tire. It would have been dangerous to stop and help, according to Dr. Anwar. The tribesmen are excellent with knives and guns and well-known for their tempers.

It was dark when we reached the Puli-Khomri Textile Club, our hotel for the night, and too late to visit the Buddhist Stupa and monastery of Takhte Rostam or the Zoroastrian Temple of Sorkh Qotal. The Textile Club is an English descendant of the British Empire with simple, but adequate, rooms and baths down the hall. A full day in the bus had worn everyone to frazzles. We went immediately in search of beer and found a small polyglot supply of Lowenbrau and Pakistani beer in the hotel bar. The entire supply was bought out before dinnertime.

Dinner was served at an immense banquet table laden with Afghani cuisine that we had become accustomed to enjoying. Everyone pulled their chairs up and cleared the platters of every scrap of food. Afterwards we retired to the surrounding smaller tables for tea, coffee and traditional music by a three-piece ensemble of drum, violin and a cross between a sitar and an autoharp. Surprisingly, some of the tour members were irked to have driven eight hours through hair-raising passes for a bountiful meal we could have had in Kabul.

The Textile Club is charming with semi-kept gardens within a walled enclosure. I have never seen a stupa and voted to get up early tomorrow morning for a 5:00 a.m. visit to Takhte Rostam. Many tour members elected to stay in bed.

Day 4
Tuesday
April 25, 1978

It was sunrise when we climbed to the crest of an impressive tepi (earth mound) to see the excavations of Takhte Rostam, a Buddhist stupa (dome-shaped monument and shrine) dating from 200 A.D. Dr. Anwar himself had been a member of the team from France and Afghanistan detailed to find the main sanctuary and surrounding courtyards. Sunlight spilled into the remains of a terrace dotted with stumps of stone columns. Down the hill, smoke from morning fires shrouded the valley, giving a bluish, imaginary quality to fields, trees, and villages protected within the bowl of mountains.

Several undisturbed tepis surround the one on which we stood, but the Afghani government has been awaiting foreign aid and archeologists to begin the formidable task of excavation. Column capitals and bases lay haphazardly around the bottom of the tepis. It was awesome to think what could be buried in these centuries of mud and rock. Someday these sites will be restored.

A pan-like fluting interrupted Dr. Anwar's monologue. The source turned out to be a young shepherd who played his haunting melody on a clay whistle shaped in a hollow triangle. The young boy was extremely handsome and photogenic so everyone took his picture. It turned out he carried a whole orchestra in his pocket—whistles of different sizes and octave ranges. He was eager to sell, first for pieces of candy or gum; then when all his shepherd buddies showed up and inflation hit, money.

We boarded to a chorus of pipings and laughter, inside and outside the bus. We tourists were trying to tame our new whistles and the shepherds were bargaining furiously before we sailed off in a cloud of dust down the road.

A tribeswoman waved shyly with her multicolored shawl from a grain field while her husband wasn't looking. When he turned around to stare at the passing bus emitting shrill pip-ings and squawks from our unruly whistles, she suddenly went inert and stared blankly into the sunrise as if we had disappeared into our dust ball.

Breakfast back at the Textile Club was improved by a lo-cal Afghan honey—dark almost molasses concoction—on our nun bread. It was delicious after our early morning hikes over tepis. We were told that two minibuses were coming to collect us for the trip to Bamiyan over "unimproved" road. That sounded ominous after our previous passages through the mountains and gut-wrenching lurches to the edge of one-lane highways.

The minibuses were late—a chronic condition in Af-ghanistan—which gave us time to explore downtown Puli-Khomri. We hired a cab with some friends. A horse-drawn cart heavily festooned with flowers, pom-poms, mirrors, bells, and ribbons thundered off with us down the main street for a quick tour of one-room sheds and stores opened for business.

Puli-Khomri consists of one thoroughfare tightly packed with shops of all descriptions. One shop—more realistically a wooden box with bulging shelves collapsing at the middle—showcased the proprietor sitting cross-legged in the center waiting to snatch down anything you pointed at, or didn't point at, just to get your attention such as heavy tribal jewelry made of silver, lapis, garnets, and agates. Another shop sold cloth, felt vests, colorful pillbox hats (some made of wild metallic fabrics), and scarves. Yet another displayed rank smelling meat hung on iron hooks in the street appreciated by a forest of flies. Several rug merchants draped maroon Bokhara wool rugs along with cotton or wool gholims (floor mats). Fabrics were violently colored orange, red, lavender, purple, green, silks, synthetics, wool, or cotton. Underneath the bland pleated chador or burqas worn by most women, there is excitement and color—red, orange, purple shoes I saw peeking out of hems. But on the street, women are formless, faceless ghosts scurrying about their daily chores.

We passed by a clothesline hung with black and gray chadoors looking like dead bats in the sunlight. Back at the Textile Club, the Mercedes minibuses were loading. We thanked our chauffeur with a big tip and patted the nose of his lathered horse. The buses were designated smoking and nonsmoking for the trip to Bamiyan. We took the last seats on the nonsmoking bus.

Bamiyan would be only two hours by air, but we spent eight hours driving over dirt or rock roads, getting stuck at the outset fording a stream for which the buses were evacuated and the men pushed. The scenery became more unbelievable as we paralleled a riverbed through canyons reminiscent of the Grand Canyon or Craters of the Moon. Blue, red, beige, and orange mountains jutted toothy pinnacles into an azure sky. We wound through gorges between endless heaps of variegated stone, the track our buses followed losing itself in washouts and recent basins carved by flash floods. Beside the river and even higher on the mountainsides, Afghani farmers had produced the impossible: verdant lime squares of new cultivation clung to the slopes contrasting with the savagery of the terrain. The beauty is stunning.

Lunch was a picnic provided by the Puli-Khomri Textile Club: cooked meat patties, two hard-boiled eggs, a boiled potato, and round nun bread with a soft drink. We stopped under the only roadside trees on the entire route. Trees seem to be a luxury. I washed my hands in a tributary to the main river and sat down to enjoy the lunch.

We spent less than an hour eating and staring at the magnificent view every way we turned. We had only just settled to eat when herdsmen arrived in small groups to cluster around the clumps of picnicking tourists. One young man, thirteen or fourteen, smiled pleasantly, and offered us a nugget looking like a goat dropping. Dr. Anwar told us it was pure hashish—resin from marijuana or hemp plants smoked or chewed as a narcotic. The boy offered to sell it to us for $11 per kilo. Dr. Anwar mentioned heroin was also readily available in these rural byways. This made us a little nervous as we finished the remains of our picnic boxes.

Back on the road, we traveled until late afternoon without a break. The view was mesmerizing immediately beside the river. Narrowing mountain passages choked by landslides put us closer and closer to the water. We passed the Red City, once an impregnable fortress carved into a burgundy mountain at the juncture of two gorges. Then along came Genghis Khan who completely destroyed the city, its inhabitants and every living thing in the surrounding countryside in retaliation for his favorite grandson's death. Historically, it seems Genghis Khan's only achievement was total annihilation. He built nothing and contributed little beyond his reputation for death and mayhem, for which he is still remembered in this fantastic valley, as a madman from the Far East.

We reached Bamiyan by dusk and checked our paralyzed rears into the Yurt Hotel, a government-owned institution of domed canvas on pole frames similar to teepees. Wind whistled through cracks between window glass and its framing, a twentieth century modification, but the accommodations were cozy, especially after our "steward," a clean-shaven Buddhist, lit the kerosene heater and the water heater. In the Yurt Hotel, we all have private showers, my first stop.

The bar is a large yurt with cushions forming a ring around the central space and a bar counter to the right of the entrance. The area is tastefully decorated with oriental rugs and cushions in maroon and red. It all makes perfect sense: if you plan to drink alcohol, why not first lay down on the floor in this beautiful womb. It beats falling down after all day in a bus jerking over rocky passes.

Dinner was similar to last night's feast but in less abundance. Most people turned in early, the exhaustion of concentrated travel already taking its toll with several ill and others borderline. Two people were confined to their rooms this evening. The food looks great and we are ravenous when it's served, but we are all experiencing various stages of loose bowels.

Large Buddha at Bamiyan with ceiling and missing leg

Day 5
Wednesday
April 26, 1978

Early morning lights the giant stone Buddhas and caves in the cliffs opposite the Yurt Hotel. It snowed on the surrounding mountains overnight. The landscape is stunning in its contrast even without the Buddhas, but the two standing statues several stories high are breathtaking. We are at a higher elevation than Puli-Khomri, yesterday, where it was actually a hot spring day.

I am nauseous and suffering diarrhea but absolutely determined to visit the Buddhas. We leave in our buses at 8:00 a.m. for the large and smaller Buddhas. The caves carved into the cliffs around the statues were the work of monks, but over intervening centuries they have been shelters for many tribes, invaders, and homeless.

The climb inside the walls to the head of the smaller Buddha gives me vertigo, perhaps because there are no guardrails or anything else to hold onto. The guide assures us they haven't lost a tourist yet as we spiral upward on narrow, serpentine stairs hollowed into the mountainside. At the top, ledges slope out and down over the Buddha, but I am not hardy enough to stay on the ledge. I get the feeling of plunging over Buddha's head in a final swan dive. Even seated, I feel compelled to slide off like in a nightmare where you can't control the tilt of the environment.

We scrambled all through the caves—low-ceilinged, austere, dark, dingy with soot from centuries of fires. In some of the central hollows, remnants of detailed and brightly painted frescoes could still be seen, unfortunately disfigured by cooking fires. Some attempts at restoration and cleaning showed the unusually delicate paintings of attitudes of Buddha that once filled these interiors.

Many photographs and backward glances later, we boarded the minibuses to travel back to the Red City, the cornerstone of two valley gorges. We ate another picnic lunch packed by the Yurt Hotel, this time eyeing everything in the box with suspicion because of the high number of tour members having difficulty with the cuisine, including myself.

The lunch was exactly like yesterday's and we ate everything. After a brief rest in the grass along the roadside, we climbed to the top of the fortress for a splendid 360-degree panorama.

The Red City is hewn out of a brilliant maroon mountain. Very little grows to distract the eye from ramparts perched on top of sheer cliffs protecting the lower and upper cities. Remnants of brick walls sit astride stone hills and gullies forming fantastic serpentine arrangements that become the citadel. The structures interlock and ascend like a child's block castle or a fortress designed on Mars.

We climbed to the upper city wall separating the citadel from a sheer drop down the rear of the fortress. Winds shrieked around destroyed buttresses and arches, hanging sentinels over the ruins. Distant mountains were frosted with light snow that drifted toward us as gentle rain. The entire group became silent at the lowering sky and primitive environment of this seemingly impregnable fortress that was ransacked and destroyed.

Dr. Anwar told us another reason Afghanis call this the Red City. When Genghis Khan came through on his rampage, he killed everything and everyone in the valley protected by the fortress. No one could stop the Mongol hordes even with this incredible structure to withstand the onslaught. A few survivors initiated the folk legend that the streets ran red with blood. Looking at this mound of rubble and its overpowering presence, the Mongols led by Genghis must have been ferocious to decimate this place.

We ran down the sheer inclines to the buses, anxious for shelter and getting drenched in the increasing downpour. The buses took us to the City of Noise directly opposite the Buddhas. By now it had begun to thunder and pour so that only the desperate or foolhardy raced to the top and back down the hillside.

The City of Noise is a spectacular ruin perched on the top of a small mountain facing the Bamiyan Buddhas. But after the Red City, it seemed anticlimactic. We should have come here first. Of course, the heavy rain didn't help either.

This evening was wet and dismal. I discovered the rain blew through the window crevice onto my pillow. We rearranged the furniture and napped before dinner in the Balkh Restaurant "downtown," immediately beside the local bazaar. No one seemed anxious to shop in the rain and in our compromised health.

The Balkh Restaurant is entered on the street by stairs descending to a cellar painted red and orange, lit by candles everywhere, and decorated with Afghan tribal artifacts and wall frescoes. The city of Balkh, near Mazar-e Sharif, the other destination we could have visited, was a prosperous stop on the oriental trade route until Genghis Khan razed it around 1220. Legend claims that Zoroaster lived in Balkh long before Alexander the Great trekked through Afghanistan.

One long banquet table accommodated everyone. Our first course was vegetable soup, a regular appetizer for all our formal meals so far. The waiters wore colorful tunics, bright skullcaps, and baggy trousers. They quickly replaced the soup course with a variety of dishes we were accustomed to eating on our trip. Everything was delicious as we devoured our meals like a pack of jackals. The evening became more lively as we sampled Afghani wines and brandy. Apparently, the country is not completely dry. I had some brandy over canasta before dinner and couldn't take any more with my weak stomach.

Everyone parted quickly for bed. We were all exhausted and anticipating another early start tomorrow morning.

Day 6
Thursday
April 27, 1978

For some reason, we decided to shower, prepare, and pack last night. This morning we dressed in 20 minutes because the water was off. We dropped off our bags at the buses on our way to a 6:30 a.m. breakfast.

I am still nauseous but much better than yesterday which was difficult getting through. If it weren't for the uniqueness of this trip, I would have preferred to stay in bed.

The water was still off after breakfast, but I insisted on using the restroom one more time, the last in a real bathroom for the next eight hours to Istaliff. We departed shortly after 7:00 a.m., the bus drivers having changed the slit tire on the nonsmoking bus. We were remarkably on time this morning.

The trip to Kabul via Istaliff took us through two passes with sensational vistas of spring-green countryside through the strange prism of Afghani sunlight. Everything seems so clear. We stopped for a leg-stretch in the first village we encountered around 10:30 while the bus drivers repaired the undercarriage of the nonsmoking bus. Yesterday we seemed to hit some potholes and rocks very hard.

The shopkeepers peddled lamé and embroidered hats, almonds, soft drinks, decorative tapes, and scarves. These were the "best prices" seen to date. I later regretted not buying a lined black velour vest heavily embroidered with gold tape and mirrors for $5.50, "first price." Who knows what could have happened after some bargaining. On our departure, several shopkeepers closed their establishments for the rest of the day, windows and doors fully shuttered as our buses barely cleared the village.

We were rattled to pieces on the dirt road until it finally rejoined the paved route we had taken to Puli-Khomri. One hour from the junction at Baghe Awghan and off the main road again, but this time on a paved secondary road, we reached the Istaliff Hotel for lunch. The hotel is pleasantly situated in a large forest garden on a rise overlooking the town, the plains we had just traversed, and the distant snow-covered Hindu Kush. The weather was cool but sunny—a perfect temperature for our return to Kabul.

Qabuli palow (rice with carrots and raisins) framed by fresh fruits, salad, and bowls of chicken and beef were welcomed by the starving crew. We ate hungrily, leaving no scraps.

Next on the itinerary was a browse through Istaliff Bazaar because Afghanis know tourists have an insatiable appetite for shopping. So far we haven't let them down. I kicked myself for not buying the vest I had seen earlier in the day. Here, a shopkeeper ("especially for you, Madam") offered me the same style for $10.00. The bazaar, famed for its glazed pottery, seemed higher priced than necessary, but some tour members found items they could afford.

On the way to Istaliff, we had noticed some fancy delta-winged jets banking overhead—an anachronism considering that people barely drove cars and trucks in these parts. In fact, we have encountered very few vehicles on the roads since we left Kabul. The closer we got to Kabul, the more we saw jets swooping and diving in the distance.

On entering the city, tanks stared us down from every intersection. Soldiers armed with machine guns or rifles with fixed bayonets observed us from housetops and walls. The photograph of the Afghani president had disappeared from its prominent displays inside shops and on public buildings.

The shoppers in our tour group had planned to be dropped off at Chicken Street on the way to the Intercontinental, our hotel for our last night in Kabul. But Chicken Street was CLOSED. We immediately drove to the Intercontinental only to be turned away at the gate by a trio of tanks and hostile soldiers who spoke gruffly to our tour leader and the drivers of the minibuses. It was then that the situation caused alarm and the photographers put away their cameras.

Dr. Anwar ran back to an intersection to ask for news from the radio station, but everything was off the air and the station was also closed. We tried to reach the American Embassy only to find that street cordoned off by more hostile soldiers brandishing guns and tanks rolling their gun barrels in our direction.

Stalled by a curb, two bus loads of 41 frightened tourists, two bus drivers, an assistant, and Dr. Anwar waited nervously while our temporarily appointed leaders conferred helplessly. Gunfire sounded in the park immediately beside us. The shots were at close proximity and panicked everyone in the buses. We huddled below windows or sat on the floor.

The driver of our nonsmoking bus tried to remove the keys from the ignition and was practically assaulted by the passengers. He laughed and sat down on the curb for a cigarette. His assistant had been alternately riding on the roof with the luggage in order to smoke. Now he sat on the curb with the driver as they smoked several cigarettes in quick succession, whispering together and avoiding eye contact with passengers.

As mortar rounds sounded in our immediate vicinity, Dr. Anwar, the drivers, and our leaders hopped on the buses and urged the drivers to hurry down a residential side street. We were all screaming and shrieking over the roaring gunfire and the straining engines of our overheated minibuses. Two blocks into this normally quiet street, the buses began turning around at the moment we were surrounded by earsplitting detonations and the clatter of rocket canisters and shells on the pavement.

Panic is a terrible feeling inside a minibus packed with passengers four abreast and no aisle for a quick exit. We understood that every second counted in these sitting-duck, red and white buses. We halted before a luridly painted sign of a bird's nest containing two eggs on what appeared to be a mountaintop above the door of a convenient hostel.

We peeled out row-by-row after the command, "Run like hell!" In a lull between detonations, another command: "Leave everything you don't absolutely need!"

We raced across the pavement and into the gate with large shell casings rattling around our feet. Everyone crammed into a modest reception room, huddling in corners, sitting on the floor, desk, coffee tables, and propped against the walls. One woman screamed repeatedly that she wanted to call the American Embassy only to be informed that the telephones were out.

Detonations continued intermittently so close that the walls rattled, the ground shook, and plaster dust sifted on our heads. It was decided to disperse the crowd into some vacant rooms and corridors of the darkened hotel. Power was also out.

We led a group of ten to a room facing an inner courtyard while the men raced out to unload the luggage from the buses before the drivers fled with the vehicles. Some luggage was abandoned on the top racks because the bombing from those lovely delta winged jets we had seen earlier was just too frightening to endure outside the confines of this small hotel. The minibuses and grim drivers sped off, never to return.

The hostel was inhabited by an international collection of young men and women, some college students, who had been traveling through India, Nepal, and farther east. They were sojourning in Afghanistan to partake of the incomparably pure hashish. Some of them were so stoned, they had no concept of what was happening outside.

One of our leaders moved our group of ten from the room where the windows were too vulnerable, into the dark, crowded corridor where everyone sat with backs against the walls. The hotel fuses were pulled to prevent anyone from accidentally turning on a light and making the establishment a target.

We crouched in the hallway, some talking quietly, others chain-smoking, one lady cradling a pocket radio waiting to translate any announcements from Farsi into English. One group clustered at the door facing the street on our end of the hall. They talked and laughed hysterically until one of the leaders shushed them with the warning that soldiers were patrolling the side streets.

Neighborhood gunfire continued sporadically late into the night.

By 8:00 p.m., the radio crackled to life with an announcement confirming a military coup and inaugurating the Democratic Republic of Afghanistan. There was a curfew and no civilians should be out on the streets. People in the streets after dark would be shot on sight, and things were under control, according to the announcer. That meant the gunfire we kept hearing was possibly aimed at people.

Dr. Anwar conferred with members of the tour. Most of us could barely stand up, our knees were knocking so. We would spend the night in the hostel and were assigned to vacant rooms, ten to a room. Most of us were damned glad to be here.

The only two bathrooms for the entire hotel were along this corridor. I made a quick trip to one of these pits before going back across the courtyard to the room we had originally vacated for the corridor. The footprint latrines were overflowing and backed up, creating a sea of feces, urine, and vomit from the drug addicts inhabiting the hotel.

My husband and I sank into a narrow wood cot with a woven string frame under the thin kapok mattress. I debated whether to take my shoes off after an abbreviated meal of beef jerky and half a local pastry someone had stashed in a bag. We were so grateful for the horded food even though no one had much of an appetite.

Leaving our shoes on in case of an emergency exit, I slept fitfully, clenching and flinching each time the jets flew overhead and released more rounds of shells into the presidential palace four blocks away, according to a knowledgeable tour member. I have never heard anything quite so disturbing as the sound of the release mechanism raining cannon rounds on buildings, the silence, then earsplitting explosions, followed by rattling walls and masonry, and sometimes screams and sobs. Then deeper silence. A military member of the group commented that he trained the pilots better than to miss their strategic targets and to dump payloads into residential areas.

Several of our room members snored so loudly in a concert that the rest of the jealous audience finally shut them up at 4:00 a.m. My watch dial was my friend.

View of large Buddha at Bamiyan

Day 7
Friday
April 28, 1978

A huge moon illuminated the courtyard, lighting the way for two women and myself as we headed for the least noxious of the latrines. We rolled up our pant legs and proceeded to business as quickly as possible. The walls were covered with hallucinogenic paintings by drugged-up students, both in the latrines and the hotel rooms. Some of the murals were pornographic. They might have been entertaining if we weren't afraid for our lives.

Gunfire from machine guns and tanks erupted in the neighborhood. We were told earlier that if a counteroffensive were attempted, it would begin at dawn and the moon certainly helped.

Back in the room, ten tightly-wound people faked sleep as jets recommenced strafing the palace and government buildings. At daybreak we got up and were given tea from the kitchen next door, a welcome comfort in the middle of chaos. Shooting finally ceased, except for a sporadic rattle. At least the jets stopped swooping over this poor little downtown, which must have been, bombed to rubble since yesterday afternoon.

We had a few strips of beef jerky left that were shared with our roommates. Some efforts were made to straighten ourselves up: brushing teeth, washing faces, combing hair. There was little anyone could do with gray cheeks and sagging eyes. We all looked like hell. The bathrooms had become entirely unusable until two tour members gallantly unclogged the latrines twice!

The radio announcer, between selections of celebratory music, called for support of the new government, no counter-coup, and a sincere effort to aid foreigners stranded in Kabul. The airport would be closed for several days due to damage sustained during the fighting. That eliminated any possibility of leaving this morning, as originally scheduled.

The proprietor charged a mere $10 per person. We thanked him profusely for opening his door to us yesterday afternoon. Then we began the process of ferrying four people at a time by taxi to the Intercontinental Hotel.

We were afraid of drawing unwanted attention to ourselves in the volatile city of Kabul.

Late in the morning, we left the hostel, "the door that opened in time," according to one tour member, after photos in front of the gate under the colorful sign. Passing the tank guarding the entrance, we were the last group to arrive at the Intercontinental before a beautiful lunch.

Our rooms had tubs, which I dove into, grateful for a soaking after taking spit baths or nothing all week. The beds, everything, looked palatial. We browsed the hotel shops stuffed with lapis, silver, gold, tribal jewelry, brass, copper, clothing, and an elaborate oriental rug concession. Between yesterday and today must be what schizophrenia feels like.

At 5:00 p.m., the tour group gathered for a meeting in the lobby. We would be marooned in Kabul at least three more days—even a week—depending upon how long it took to repair the airport runways. At $60 per night without food, that was a problem for many of our tour members. Our "vacation," billed as seven days and six nights, was officially over having blown up in our faces. People were free to find cheaper accommodations than the Intercontinental if they wanted.

We decided to stay at the Intercontinental because it seemed more secure with tanks around the perimeter. Two meals per day and sharing pots of tea and coffee with our friends would cut some costs.

We learned that the palace was completely destroyed along with half the neighboring French Embassy. Water mains, cars, tanks, and Ariana's Kabul Hotel office were bombed. The former president, his family, and supporters were all shot. A new leader, Taraki, was released from jail to head a government backed by the military. The telephones were still out and the U.S. Embassy was located on a street near the palace, which was off limits. It was darkly humorous that our group included Tehran embassy and military personnel, but we could get no assistance from our own embassy in Kabul that frequently sent officials to Tehran to buy supplies from our commissary.

Dinner was a special buffet put on by the Intercontinental in place of a farewell banquet we would have had the previous night at the Golden Lotus Restaurant. The food was delicious and we all ate too much. Included were all the Afghan specialties we had grown to love in our travels in and around Kabul.

We retired early, completely exhausted, and anxious about when we would be able to leave. Fortunately, we had brought a credit card so running out of cash was not a problem. But others on our tour were already broke and planning to move out tomorrow morning.

Arches within Red City

Day 8
Saturday
April 29, 1978

We stayed at the Intercontinental for two more days, wandering around its safe preserve. The airport was finally repaired enough for a plane to take us out. Under immense military scrutiny and multiple baggage checks, we finally boarded and the plane taxied out. Everyone cheered, clapped, and cried as it took off.

We were photographed deplaning in Tehran as the first group of civilians to leave Kabul since the coup. The photograph appeared in the local newspaper.

In December 1979, the Soviets invaded Afghanistan and plunged the region into decades of war. According to news reports, in the preceding April, 1978 coup, an estimated 10,000 people died in a military-backed installation of a pro-Communist regime.

View of smaller Buddha at Bamiyan

Tour Photos
of Afghanistan

The following photos are a sampling of the many taken during the tour showing the places and people of Afghanistan. Unfortunately, many of the photos we took are not included here for a number of reasons. Some do not reproduce well due to age or content. Others include people whom we were unable to contact to obtain their permission for inclusion.

Most of the photos show a country of amazing colors and friendly people. It was springtime and people were pleasant and accommodating to our tour group.

View of Kabul from Intercontinental Hotel

View of Kabul suburb from Intercontinental Hotel

Downtown Kabul

Carpet shop on Chicken Street

Chicken Street with tourists

Shop selling chairs and pitchers on Chicken Street

Fabric store on Chicken Street

Bread store

Motorized rickshaw

*Young man and boy
on Chicken Street*

Chicken Street traffic

Young girls in colorful dress

Tribal encampment at base of mountains

Tribal walk through fields

Tribal encampment with camels

Walled fortress on hilltop

Fortified village along road to Khyber Pass

Children herding goats

Cattle herders in Afghani countryside

Pennie at Kyhber Pass frontier sign

Baby girl at Khyber Pass

Colorful overloaded bus in Djelalabad

Border buses and traffic cop

Two men at 'Bye Bye' sign

Border signs

Woman selling water

Streambed beside highway

Tourists along road near Khyber Pass

*Donkey transport
through mountains*

Two lovely young girls

Springhar Hotel courtyard

*Banquet
arrangement
and servings*

Bamiyan route, Hindu Kush, village on hillside

Road through snowy mountain pass

Market kiosk at tea time

Fruit kiosk

Market kiosk with proprietor

Boy on donkey with yellow bird

Crowded bus with passengers on top

Child doing homework at vest shop

Village clinging to snowy mountain

Rough road along rocks and fields

Hindu Kush Range

Hindu Kush Range behind a green valley

Beautiful village framed by Hindu Kush

Stupas at dawn with village below

Young boy with whistle at stupas

Horse drawn cart at roundabout

Drink stand with turbaned proprietor

Young girl holding a baby

Camel train through town

Buses stuck in stream on route to Bamiyan

Road through valley on route to Bamiyan

Bamiyan arrival showing caves carved into wall

Yurt hotel at dawn

View of Bamiyan caves for monks

*Pennie & Doug
at the Large
Buddha*

*Tourists on ledge
overlooking
Buddha's head*

Exterior cave view

Bamiyan cave frescoes of Buddhas

Bamiyan Buddhas viewed from City of Noise

Pennie at view of Red City turret

Pennie and Doug at the hostel

Intercontinental Hotel view of Kabul

Overview of
Afghanistan History

100,000 B.C.E.

    Paleolithic evidence of human tools possibly fabri-
cated by Neanderthals was unearthed in the 1970s at
archaeological sites 150 miles southwest of Kabul.

50,000 B.C.E.

    Stone implements from this era were found in
northeast Afghanistan.

35,000 – 15,000 B.C.E.

    A hunting society left numerous varieties of stone
tools in Paleolithic locales along the Hindu Kush
foothills.

20,000 – 15,000 B.C.E.

    Finely crafted tools were created near Balkh.

17,000 B.C.E.

    A small limestone rock carved with a human face is
the oldest humanoid talisman yet found in Asia.

9000 B.C.E.

    Neolithic herders roamed and farmed the foothills of
Afghanistan.

2000 B.C.E.

Bronze Age settlements traded with Indus Valley colonies. Remnants of a fertility goddess cult have been unearthed near Kandahar.

3000 – 1000 B.C.E.

Lapis lazuli was traded throughout the area. Afghanistan became a crossroads for trade and invaders.

2000 – 1500 B.C.E.

Aryan tribes from Central Asia invaded and settled across modern Iran, Afghanistan, and India.

900 – 600 B.C.E.

Zoroaster (Zarathustra) was reputedly born in Balkh and died there during a raid by northern tribes. The sage originated Zoroastrianism (an eternal battle between cosmic powers of good and evil) which was widely practiced throughout the Persian Empire, including Afghanistan, into northern India.

550 - 530 B.C.E.

Cyrus the Great of Persia spread the Achaemenid Empire and Zoroastrianism as its national faith.

330 – 150 B.C.E.

Alexander the Great conquered Afghanistan in his campaign to rule the known world, spread Hellenic culture, and rout Darius III who was murdered near the Caspian Sea.

329 B.C.E.

>Alexander founded Alexandria of Arachosia (Kandahar) on the main trade route between India and Europe.

327 B.C.E.

>After a bloody campaign, Alexander conquered Bactria (northern Afghanistan) and married Roxane, daughter of a Bactrian noble and reputed to be one of the most beautiful women in the world, in a ceremony at Balkh which was renamed Alexandria.

320 B.C.E.

>Thousands of Greek colonists joined some 13,000 Greek troops left in Bactria in a peaceful migration encouraged by Seleucus, a Macedonian general who took over Afghanistan and other eastern territories after Alexander's death.

320 B.C.E. – 650 C.E.

>The Mauryan, Kushan, and Sassanian Empires ruled Afghanistan successively.

200 B.C.E.

>The Silk Road emerged as a trade route between China and Europe, with Bactria at its midpoint, and continued in use for 1700 years.

100 C.E. – 500 C.E.

>Buddhism became widespread in Afghanistan and Asia.

300

The first standing Buddha was carved into a cliff at Bamian, home to a Buddhist community of nearly 8000 monks who lived in caves carved into the adjoining mountainside.

500

The second standing Buddha was sculpted in the Bamian cliff.

651

Arab armies brought Islam to Afghanistan twenty years after Mohammed's death. They occupied lands from Herat to Balkh.

700 – 960

Islamic rule stretched from Spain through Asia, sweeping away remnants of Zoroastrianism, Hinduism, and Buddhism in Afghanistan.

998 – 1030

Mahmud of Ghazni (southwest of Kabul) ruled the Ghaznavid Empire, a Moslem dynasty centered in Afghanistan and stretching into India, Iran, and Baluchistan.

1151 – 1215

The Ghurid dynasty ruled Afghanistan, destroyed Ghazni, and created a capital at Herat.

1215 – 1221

Khorasanians from Samarkand overran the Ghurid Empire. Power, loot, glory, and religion motivated all these invasions. The Silk Road was also a lure.

1221 – 1282

Genghis Khan swept through Afghanistan massacring its people and devastating cities and farms. After Genghis Khan's death in 1227, his descendents continued Mongol rule in an empire spanning from Hungary to China, Siberia to India. Jaghatai Khan ruled Kabul and Ghazni.

1364 – 1405

Tamerlane (Timur the Lame) invaded Afghanistan and India, establishing his empire ruled from Samarkand.

1497 – 1530

Babur conquered Afghanistan and northern India, ruling his Mughal Empire from Kabul and Ghazni. His empire lasted 200 years.

1736 – 1747

Nadir Shah, a former camel herder and bandit, ruled Persia, Afghanistan, and India from which he looted the Peacock Throne.

1747 – 1772

Ahmed Khan Abdali, commander of Nadir Shah's bodyguards, was elected shah by placing two wheat stalks in his turban. The wheat motif appeared in several Afghani national flags. Ahmed Shah's family, dubbed Durrani (pearls), became the ruling elite of Afghanistan until 1978.

ca.1750

Maritime trade routes reduced the importance of the Silk Road.

ca.1760

The British Empire increased its power and control in India along with the East India Company, founded in 1600 by Queen Elizabeth I to transfer wealth from Asia to England.

1772

Timur Shah took over upon his father's death.

1818 –1839

Timur Shah's many sons and clan members struggled for domination in numerous civil wars.

1826 – 1863

Dost Mohammed Khan ruled, with interruptions, from Kabul.

1838

The "Great Game" between Russian and British imperial expansion schemes commenced with an envoy from Russia to Dost Mohammed and lasted over a century.

1839 – 1842

The First Anglo-Afghan War was initially won by British forces in an easy takeover but lost in a massacre of remaining troops attempting a retreat to India. The British retaliated with the "Army of Retribution" to retrieve their prisoners.

1878 – 1880

The Second Anglo-Afghan War resulted after Emir Sher Ali, Dost Mohammed's son, agreed to Russian soldiers being stationed in Afghanistan. Britain demanded their mission also be stationed in Kabul. The Emir delayed his reply provoking a British attack and conquest of areas that became Pakistan. Afghanis rebelled and defeated the British at Maiwand resulting in a withdrawal of British forces.

1880 – 1901

Abdur Rahman Khan reigned by crushing opposition over what became modern territorial Afghanistan.

1884

A British and Russian commission designated Afghanistan's northern border.

1887 – 1888

Afghanistan's northwestern and western borders were finalized.

1891 – 1895

Afghanistan's northeastern border was drawn to prevent contact between British and Russian territories, resulting in Afghani terrain along the Hindu Kush.

1893

Mortimer Durand, Indian foreign secretary, was sent to Kabul to establish the Durand Line that arbitrarily separated towns and tribes between India and Afghanistan.

1901 – 1919

Habibullah Khan reigned until his assassination. Amanullah Khan succeeded his father and declared Afghanistan independent of Britain. He then declared a jihad (holy war) against the British that triggered the Third Anglo-Afghan War confirming Afghanistan's independence. The Treaty of Rawalpindi was signed August 18, 1919, celebrated as Liberation Day.

1921

Afghanistan signed a Treaty of Friendship with Russia and Vladimir Lenin donated 13 planes with pilots to create Afghanistan's air force.

1923

Afghanistan's first constitution provided for a hereditary kingship, an appointed cabinet, and a partially elected parliament.

1929 – 1933

After King Amanullah's exile and a civil war, Nadir Shah ruled until his assassination.

1933 – 1973

Muhammad Zahir Shah, Nadir Shah's son, ruled for 40 years until he was deposed by Daoud Khan, his cousin.

1941

Britain and Russia together invaded neighboring Iran and deposed its shah who had declined to deport German agents. Britain and Russia demanded Afghanistan ban German agents resulting in Afghani expulsion of most international advisers and a declaration of neutrality in World War II, like Afghanistan's neutral status in World War I.

1947

Britain withdrew from India and partitioned the subcontinent into Pakistan and India. Pakistan immediately closed its western border with Afghanistan, increasing border disputes over a demarcation never fully accepted by Afghanistan.

1969

Famine killed approximately 100,000 Afghanis.

1973

While visiting Europe, King Zahir was deposed and
exiled in a coup by Daoud Khan.

1978

On April 17, Mir Akbar Khyber, a Parcham party
organizer, was murdered. His funeral became an
anti-American demonstration of thousands of people
closing Kabul streets. Daoud Khan arrested and jailed
leaders of the People's Democratic Party of Afghanistan, provoking a military coup on April 27 – 28.
Daoud Khan and his family were executed. Air Force
Colonel Abdul Qadir Dagarwal ordered air strikes to
bomb the royal palace in Kabul. An estimated 10,000
died in the Communist coup known as the Saur (April)
Revolution. Nur Muhammad Taraki became the
leader of Afghanistan. April 28 was subsequently
celebrated as Revolution Day.

1979

In February, Adolf Dubs, American Ambassador, was
kidnapped and killed in a rescue attempt. In March, a
rebel uprising murdered approximately 100 Russian
advisers and their family members whose heads were
displayed on stakes and paraded through Herat.
"Shabnamah" (night letters), underground newslet-
ters, were circulated in Kabul. In September, Hafizul-
lah Amin arrested Taraki who later died under suspi-
cious circumstances. Amin was killed during the So-

viet invasion of Kabul in December. Babrak Karmal became president.

1980

Russian invaders were challenged by growing resistance similar to Britain's experiences in three Anglo-Afghan wars. Mullahs called for jihad against the occupiers. Thousands of "mujahidin" (holy warriors) answered the call.

1984

Osama bin Laden began his fundraising for and participation in Afghani resistance fighting. His organization, al Qaeda (the Base), took root in Afghanistan.

1986

Babrak Karmal resigned and lived in exile in Moscow until his death. His former bodyguard, Muhammad Najibullah, became president with endorsement from Russia. The Soviets began withdrawal of their troops from Afghanistan.

1989

After a decade of war, the Soviets completed their withdrawal from Afghanistan.

1992

President Najibullah resigned and took refuge in the United Nations compound in Kabul. The Taliban executed him in 1996.

1992 – 1996

Mujahidin warlords ruled regions of Afghanistan.

1993

Terrorists schooled in Afghani training camps bombed the World Trade Center.

1996

The Taliban ruled from Kabul.

1998

August 7 marked the bombing of United States' embassies in Kenya and Tanzania. Bin Laden's followers were blamed, and the U.S. bombed installations in Afghanistan.

2000

Al Qaeda took credit for bombing the USS Cole in Yemen.

2001

In March, the Taliban blasted the two standing Buddhas in Bamian. The Taliban next destroyed 3000 or more artworks considered pagan at the Kabul Museum. On September 11, al Qaeda agents flew planes into the World Trade Center in New York City and the Pentagon in Washington, D.C., killing approximately 3000 people. In October, the U.S. bombed Osama bin Laden's camps in Afghanistan. In December, the Taliban ceded power to an interim government headed by Hamid Karzai.

2002

The U.S. began a "war on terror" to end Taliban and
al Qaeda attacks of global jihad. Mercenary soldiers
staffed covert CIA contracts.

2004

In April the missing Bactrian gold, 20,000 ancient artifacts, were recovered. In October, Afghanistan held
democratic elections confirming Hamid Karzai president of the Islamic republic.

2007

Opium production rapidly increased providing over 90
percent of the world's heroin and morphine while
funding a Taliban resurgence.

Bibliography

—Delong, Michael, and Noah Lukeman, <u>Inside CentCom</u>. Washington, D.C.: Regnery Publishing, Inc., 2004.

—Ewans, Martin, <u>Afghanistan: A Short History of Its People and Politics.</u> New York: Harper-Collins Publishers, Inc., 2002.

—Jones, Ann, <u>Kabul in Winter</u>. New York: Metropolitan Books, 2006.

—Lawler, Andrew. "Saving Afghan Treasures." <u>National Geographic</u> December 2004: 24-41.

—Roy, Oliver, <u>The New Central Asia</u>. New York: New York University Press, 2007.

—Schultheis, Rob, <u>Night Letters: Inside Wartime Afghanistan</u>. Guilford: The Lyons Press, 1992.

—Tanner, Stephen, <u>Afghanistan</u>. Philadelphia: Da Capo Press, 2002.

—Wahab, Shaista, and Barry Youngerman, <u>A Brief History of Afghanistan</u>. New York: Facts On File, Inc., 2007.

—Wikipedia: The Free Encyclopedia. "Abdul Qadir Dagarwal." Available online. URL: http//en.wikipedia.org/wiki/Abdul_Qadir_Dagarwal. Updated June 4, 2009.

—Wikipedia: The Free Encyclopedia. "People's Democratic Party of Afghanistan." Available online. URL: http//en.wikipedia.org/wiki/People%27s_Democratic_Party_of_Af ghanistan. Updated June 11, 2009.

—Willis, Terri, <u>Afghanistan</u>. New York: Children's Press, Scholastic, Inc., 2008.

—Yasgar, Batya Swift, <u>Behind the Burqa</u>. Hoboken: John Wiley & Sons, Inc., 2002.

About The Author

Penelope Rundle was born in Atlanta, Georgia, and grew up in Bangladesh, Europe, Somalia, and Trinidad and Tobago. She studied French language and literature at the Sorbonne, Paris, France. She earned a bachelor's degree in French and journalism, and a master's degree in Spanish from Simmons College, Boston, Massachusetts. After returning from Iran to Boston, she earned a law degree from Suffolk University and a master of public health from Harvard. She has worked as a parent, writer, teacher, and lawyer.